What causes tsunamis? Who studies earthquakes? How do volcanoes form? What should people do if an avalanche hits?

Find out the answers to these questions and more in . . .

Magic Tree House®
Research Guide
TSUNAMIS
and Other Natural Disasters

A nonfiction companion to
High Tide in Hawaii

It's Jack and Annie's very own guide to geological disasters.

Including:

• Tsunami warning signs
• Earthquake safety
• The eruption of Mount Saint Helens
• Volcanologists

And much more!

Magic Tree House® Research Guide

TSUNAMIS
and Other Natural Disasters

A nonfiction companion to
High Tide in Hawaii

by Mary Pope Osborne
and Natalie Pope Boyce

illustrated by Sal Murdocca

A STEPPING STONE BOOK™
Random House 🏠 New York

Published in the United States by Random House Children's Books,
a division of Random House, Inc., New York.

RANDOM HOUSE and colophon are registered trademarks and A STEPPING STONE
BOOK and colophon are trademarks of Random House, Inc. MAGIC TREE HOUSE
is a registered trademark of Mary Pope Osborne; used under license.

www.magictreehouse.com
www.randomhouse.com/kids

Educators and librarians, for a variety of teaching tools, visit us at
www.randomhouse.com/teachers

Library of Congress Cataloging-in-Publication Data
Osborne, Mary Pope.
Tsunamis and other natural disasters : a nonfiction companion to High tide in
Hawaii / by Mary Pope Osborne and Natalie Pope Boyce ;
illustrated by Sal Murdocca. — 1st ed.
    p.   cm. — (Magic tree house research guide) "A stepping stone book."
Includes bibliographical references and index.
ISBN 978-0-375-83221-5 (trade) — ISBN 978-0-375-93221-2 (lib. bdg.)
1. Tsunamis—Juvenile literature. 2. Natural disasters—Juvenile literature.
3. Vesuvius (Italy)—Eruption, 79—Juvenile literature. I. Boyce, Natalie Pope.
II. Murdocca, Sal. III. Title. IV. Series.
GC221.5O83 2007   363.34'95—dc22   2005024663

Printed in the United States of America
10 9 8 7 6 5 4 3 2 1
First Edition

For the Viking, Elaine O. Boyce

Scientific Consultant:
LISA WALD, Education and Outreach Coordinator, U.S. Geological Survey.

Education Consultant:
HEIDI JOHNSON, Earth Science and Paleontology, Lowell Junior High School, Bisbee, Arizona.

Very special thanks to Paul Coughlin for his photographs; and to the supportive team at Random House: Joanne Yates Russell, Gloria Cheng, Mallory Loehr; and especially to the ever-patient, ever-kind Angela Roberts and Diane Landolf.

TSUNAMIS
and Other Natural Disasters

Contents

Dear Readers,

We saw on television how the horrible tsunami of 2004 took so many lives and destroyed so much property. We realized that we didn't know exactly what caused tsunamis. Then we started to talk about other disasters. We knew a little about volcanoes and earthquakes, but not enough. We had seen pictures of landslides and avalanches, but we needed to know exactly why and how they occur. So we decided to write a book about natural disasters like these.

Our research took a lot of time. But the good news is that there is tons of helpful

material out there. There were hundreds of excellent Web sites about natural disasters. And there were loads of books in the library. In fact, we had almost too much information. We sat down and discussed what we had learned. We filled many notebooks and wore down lots of pencils. We spent hours printing out articles and pictures. Whew! It was a lot of work. But it was also really fun. We still say that doing research is like taking vitamins for the brain!

Jack
Annie

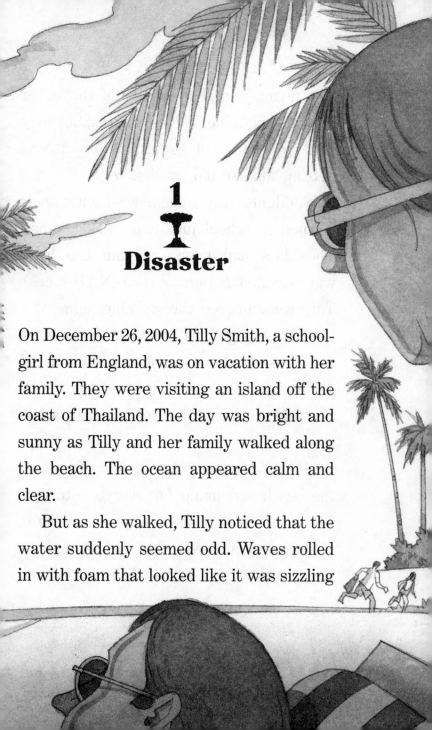

1

Disaster

On December 26, 2004, Tilly Smith, a school-girl from England, was on vacation with her family. They were visiting an island off the coast of Thailand. The day was bright and sunny as Tilly and her family walked along the beach. The ocean appeared calm and clear.

But as she walked, Tilly noticed that the water suddenly seemed odd. Waves rolled in with foam that looked like it was sizzling in a frying pan. The surface of the water seemed to bubble. Waves came in, but they didn't go back out again. The beach was getting smaller and smaller.

Suddenly Tilly remembered what she'd learned in school just two weeks before. The class had been studying the huge waves called *tsunamis* (tsoo-NAH-meez). Tilly remembered the warning signs of a tsunami. She got really scared. These were the signs she'd learned about! She started screaming. Tilly's parents ran to her side. She told them what her teacher had said in class.

Tilly and her parents rushed up and down the beach screaming for everyone to run. Then they raced to warn people in the hotel. Everyone scrambled for safety. Tilly and her family climbed to the third floor of the hotel.

Minutes later, a wall of water crashed onto the beach. Three huge tsunami waves struck, one after the other. The sea seemed like an angry monster. Everything in its path was gobbled up. Tables and chairs landed in the pool. Palm trees toppled over.

But Tilly and her family were safe. The water did not destroy the hotel. Thanks to Tilly and her parents, many other people survived as well.

Tilly Smith meets former president Bill Clinton on a visit to the UN in 2005.

Tilly had been part of a terrible *natural disaster* (dih-ZASS-tur). This disaster was caused by an earthquake many miles away.

The earthquake took place in the Indian Ocean. It set off one of the worst tsunamis in history. Two hours after the earthquake,

A boat landed on Nataya Pumsi's house in Thailand during the tsunami.

giant waves hit the coasts of Thailand and Indonesia. Hours later, waves reached the coasts of southern India and East Africa, more than 5,000 miles away.

When it was over, around 300,000 people were dead. Two months later, rescue teams were still finding over 500 bodies a day.

Natural Disasters

Tsunamis, earthquakes, and volcanoes can create natural disasters—terrible events caused by nature. Weather causes some natural disasters like hurricanes and tornadoes. But tsunamis, earthquakes, and volcanoes begin deep inside the earth.

For many years, scientists knew little about the way the earth worked. They could not explain the exact reasons for earthquakes, tsunamis, and volcanoes. They were puzzled about why these things happened in some places and not in others.

The scientists did research for many years. Then forty years ago, a group of scientists came up with some ideas. These ideas came from clues they saw on the ocean floor. What they concluded may be hard to believe. They said that the ground we stand on is actually *floating*! And it's *moving*! These movements can cause major natural disasters.

Turn the page to find out more about the word <u>disaster</u>.

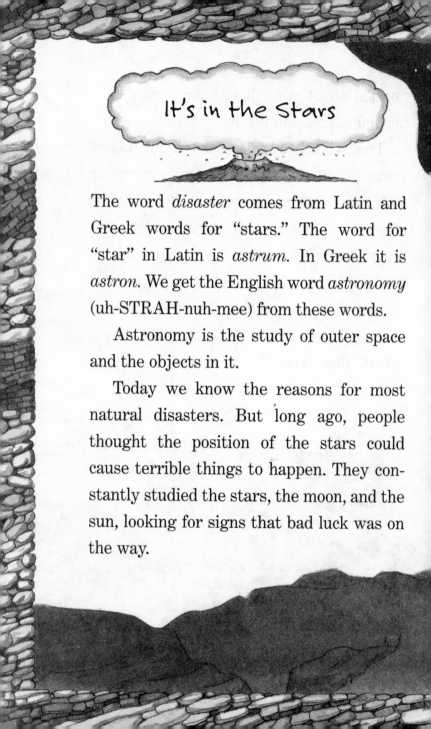

It's in the Stars

The word *disaster* comes from Latin and Greek words for "stars." The word for "star" in Latin is *astrum*. In Greek it is *astron*. We get the English word *astronomy* (uh-STRAH-nuh-mee) from these words.

Astronomy is the study of outer space and the objects in it.

Today we know the reasons for most natural disasters. But long ago, people thought the position of the stars could cause terrible things to happen. They constantly studied the stars, the moon, and the sun, looking for signs that bad luck was on the way.

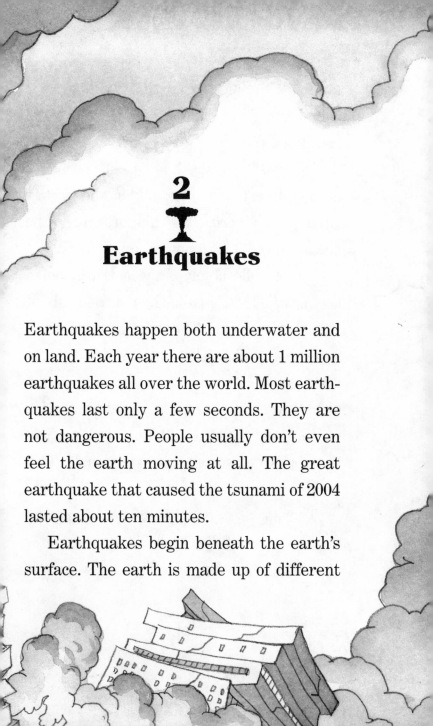

2

Earthquakes

Earthquakes happen both underwater and on land. Each year there are about 1 million earthquakes all over the world. Most earthquakes last only a few seconds. They are not dangerous. People usually don't even feel the earth moving at all. The great earthquake that caused the tsunami of 2004 lasted about ten minutes.

Earthquakes begin beneath the earth's surface. The earth is made up of different layers. The outer layer that we live on is called the *crust*. The crust is made up of rocks and dirt.

In most places, the crust is about twenty-five miles thick under the earth's surface. The crust is thinner under the ocean. There it is about six miles thick.

The middle layer of the earth is called the *mantle* (MAN-tul). The mantle is about 1,800 miles thick. The mantle consists of super-hot rocks. These rocks are not exactly solid. But they're not exactly liquid, either. Rocks in the mantle are like a thick paste. Deeper down in the mantle, many of the rocks get so hot that they melt. This melted rock is called *magma*.

There are two parts of the core, the deepest layer of the earth. There is an *outer core* and an *inner core*. The outer core is about 1,400 miles thick. It is made up of melted rocks and metal (mostly iron and nickel).

The inner core is about the size of our moon. It is mostly made up of super-hot metals. The temperature of the inner core can be over 6,000 degrees. That's hotter than anything you can imagine!

Even though the inner core is very hot, there is so much pressure on it that the metals remain solid.

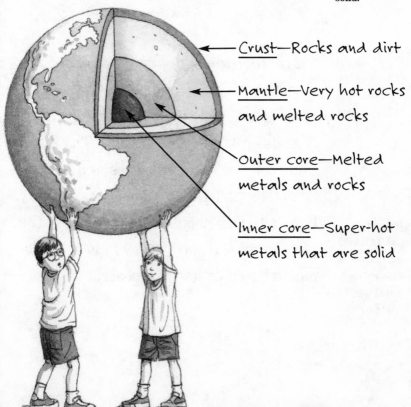

Crust—Rocks and dirt

Mantle—Very hot rocks and melted rocks

Outer core—Melted metals and rocks

Inner core—Super-hot metals that are solid

How is the earth like a peach?

That's easy! The skin is li[ke] the crust; the fruit is lik[e] the mantle; and the pit is like the core.

Plate Tectonic Theory

Scientists have found that the earth's crust is not made up of one solid piece. It is made up of different sections. These sections come in different sizes and shapes. Scientists call the sections *plates*. They have a theory about the plates called the *plate tectonic theory*. A *theory* is an explanation based on lots of research.

Tectonic (tek-TAHN-ik) comes from a Greek word that means "builder."

26

Nine large plates and many smaller plates form the crust. Scientists describe the plates as huge platforms of rock and dirt. They fit together a little bit like a jigsaw puzzle. The platforms, or plates, actually float on top of the mantle.

Scientists have concluded that the plates move. Experts believe the moving plates cause earthquakes and volcanoes. They also believe that the moving plates created some of our great mountains.

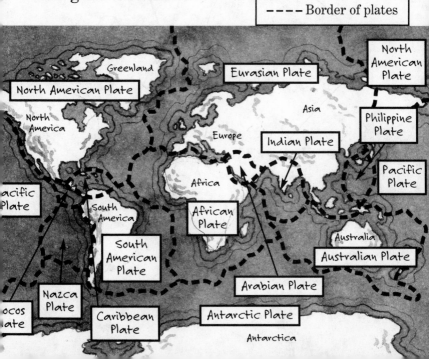

---- Border of plates

North American Plate

Greenland

Eurasian Plate

North American Plate

North America

Asia

Philippine Plate

Europe

Indian Plate

Pacific Plate

Africa

Pacific Plate

South America

African Plate

Australia

Australian Plate

South American Plate

Arabian Plate

Nazca Plate

Antarctic Plate

ocos late

Caribbean Plate

Antarctica

Movement of the Plates

The plates move very slowly. In fact, they move about as slowly as your fingernails grow. When moving plates meet, three things can happen.

Some plates slide past each other. When they slip past, they rub against each other. When plates move away from one another, it is called <u>rifting</u>.

At times, the plates collide. Sometimes when this happens, one plate slides under the other. This is called <u>subduction</u> (sub-DUK-shun).

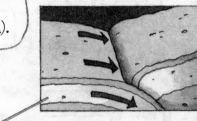

What Causes Earthquakes?

The point directly above where an earth-quake occurs is the *epicenter* (EP-uh-sen-tur). The epicenter is often at the edge of moving plates. As the plates slide past each other, they cause a break in the earth's sur-face. This break is called a *fault*.

The San Andreas Fault is over 1,000 miles long.

When the plates move, rocks break off. This creates edges that are rough and jagged. As the plates continue to move, the edges of one plate can get stuck on the edges of the other.

When the edges come unstuck, a huge amount of energy is suddenly released. This powerful force causes the earth to shake. These movements are called *seismic* (SIZE-mik) *waves*. *Seismic* means that the movements are caused by an earthquake.

A huge earthquake releases about the same amount of energy as 25,000 atomic bombs!

Earthquake waves move on average about 16,000 miles per hour through rock. The waves move fastest through colder rock. They slow down in sand, water, and warmer rocks.

During a big earthquake, the ground seems to turn into jelly. The earth shakes from side to side and rolls like waves in the ocean. Sometimes the earth cracks. Cars bounce up and down. Windows break. Buildings crumble, sometimes trapping people inside. Entire cities can tumble into ruins after only a few minutes of shaking.

Following an earthquake, *aftershocks* can occur for days, weeks, and even months.

Aftershocks are smaller quakes set off by the main quake.

If you are ever in an earthquake, you'll never forget it!

Did you know there are earthquakes on the moon?

Yes, but they are actually moonquakes!

How Earthquakes Happen
Plates move
Collide
Pull apart
Brush together
Slide under one another
Energy released

Scientists who study earthquakes are called seismologists (size-MAHL-uh-jistz).

Measuring Earthquakes

Scientists use an instrument called a *seismograph* (SIZE-muh-graf) to measure movements deep inside the earth. There are seismographs all over the world.

Seismologists know an earthquake is under way when the seismograph records rapid, strong movement near the edge of a plate.

Experts describe an earthquake's strength by using numbers on the *moment magnitude* (MAG-nuh-tood) *scale.* The earthquake that caused the 2004 tsunami was a magnitude 9.3.

Magnitude means "the size of an event."

Scientists use numbers on the scale to describe how hard the earth shakes.

Great: 8 and larger
Major: 7–7.9
Strong: 6–6.9
Medium: 5–5.9
Light: 4–4.9
Minor: 3–3.9

Earthquake!

Not all earthquakes create tsunamis. Earthquakes happen on land as well as underwater. Some of the most powerful earthquakes have been on land. They have killed thousands of people and destroyed whole cities.

California and Alaska have the most earthquakes in the United States.

In 1906, a terrible earthquake nearly destroyed the city of San Francisco, California. The epicenter was near the downtown. The shaking only lasted about a minute.

Buildings began to collapse. Victims were trapped under the rubble. As the buildings toppled, they killed people in the streets. Gas lines broke. Terrible fires raged out of control. Firemen ran out of water. To stop the fires from spreading from building to building, firefighters blew up some of the buildings with dynamite.

34

As fires spread through the damaged city, people began to flee for their lives. They tried to carry all their belongings with them. Some used baby buggies, wagons, and go-carts. Others carried trunks and suit-cases. The loads were too heavy for many. Soon trunks and household items littered the roads. Many people lost everything they owned. Much of the city was a smoking ruin.

San Francisco, 1906

It took years after the earthquake before San Francisco returned to normal. Today it

Earthquake Safety

Predicting an earthquake is not like predicting the weather. Even with good instruments, no one can tell exactly when an earthquake will hit. And no one is sure how much damage will result. You will probably never be in an earthquake. But if you are, and you feel the ground shaking, do these things right away!

1. Take cover under a table, in a doorway, or in a closet.

2. Stay away from heavy objects that

is a beautiful city that tourists visit from all over the world.

could topple over, such as bookcases and re-frigerators.

3. If you are outside, get away from buildings and power lines.

4. If you hear a hissing sound or smell gas, leave quickly!

Chang Hen's Urn

About 1,800 years ago in ancient China, a man named Chang Hen designed a special urn to measure earthquakes.

The urn had eight dragon heads on top, each with a ball in its mouth. Eight frogs with open mouths sat beneath.

When the ground shook, so did the urn. One or more balls fell into the frogs' mouths. When Chang Hen saw a ball had fallen, he concluded there had been an earthquake. He thought he could tell how strong the quake was by the number of balls in the frogs' mouths. He thought he could tell where the epicenter was by which side of the urn the balls were on.

Chang Hen's urn could actually show that the earth had moved. It could also give an idea about how strong the movement was. But it took thousands of years before scientists could tell exactly where an earthquake's epicenter was and how strong the quake had been.

This is a modern model of Chang Hen's urn.

3
Tsunamis

Tsunami means "harbor wave" in Japanese. Some people call tsunamis "tidal waves." But tides do not create waves. Most waves come from wind moving over water. Tsunami waves come from deep down in the ocean.

They are usually caused by underwater earthquakes or landslides, or volcanoes near or under the sea.

Events like these change the ocean

Meteorites and asteroids landing in the ocean can create tsunamis, too.

floor. They force a huge amount of water up to the surface. Waves begin to spread out in all directions. They travel very quickly, some as fast as 500 miles per hour or more!

A normal wave travels about fifty-six miles per hour.

In fact, if Alaska were rocked by a quake, a tsunami could reach Tokyo faster than a jet plane!

It's faster than a jet plane!

But if you were in the middle of the ocean during a tsunami, you would scarcely notice a ripple. In the open ocean, tsunami waves are usually only one to two feet higher than normal waves. Sailors rarely notice any change when the waves pass under their boats.

Tsunamis Hit the Shore

When tsunami waves reach land, scientists say the waves begin to "feel the ocean bottom." The waves start to slow down. But as they slow down, they grow in height. It's just like a traffic jam. When cars are bumper to bumper, if a speeding car plows into them, a huge chain of crashes occurs. The waves begin to bunch up together. A 2-foot wave can become a 200-foot wall of water! That's as tall as a ten-story building!

There may be as many as ten waves in a series. The waves follow anywhere from ten to ninety minutes apart.

The height of a tsunami wave compared to normal sea level is called the <u>run-up</u>.

Good job, Tilly! You paid attention in class!

Most people think a tsunami looks like a huge wave. But from the shore, the ocean's surface looks flat. People can't tell that danger is rushing toward them.

Sometimes there are clues that a tsunami is on the way. One clue is that the water pulls back a long way from shore. This is called a *drawback*. But sometimes the tide surges in and doesn't go back out again. The water seems to bubble and foam. Boats close to shore bob violently up and down. Tilly Smith saw some of these things and knew trouble was on the way.

Tsunami Damage

A strong tsunami can cause major destruction. When the waves hit, the force can kill people as they try to flee. Many drown as they struggle in the water. Others are sucked out to sea as the waves retreat. Five days after the 2004 tsunami, a woman named Malawati was found alive clinging to a palm tree. She was a hundred miles out to sea!

Malawati was brought to a hospital in Malaysia after her rescue.

Homes, buildings, and roads wash away. Electricity lines are downed. When the tsunami is over, it leaves behind tons of litter. Trees, mud, garbage, and even bodies are everywhere. And to make things worse,

A boy sits by the ruins of his village in Sri Lanka after the 2004 tsunami.

sometimes the water floods areas where tanks filled with chemicals, oil, and gasoline are stored. It also breaks sewer lines. When these things happen, the water becomes polluted. People are at high risk for illness and infection.

Tsunami Warning

In 1964, a tsunami hit Alaska and Hawaii. After that happened, U.S. scientists created a tsunami warning system.

Since earthquakes cause most tsunamis, seismographs are a big part of the warning system. Seismographs record the strength of the quake. The scientists also put satellites in orbit to keep track of the height of the ocean.

There are few tsunamis in the Indian Ocean, and no warning system was in place for the 2004 tsunami.

Since most tsunamis in the United States happen in Hawaii, that state has an excellent warning system. There are also systems in place in Alaska, California, Oregon, and Washington State.

There are usually several hours between the earthquake and the time a tsunami

Tsunami Safety

1. If you are on the beach and hear sirens, run to higher ground as fast as you can!

2. If you have time when you leave your home, take water, food, a portable radio with batteries, and a good flashlight.

3. Listen to the radio. Don't go back home until you hear it is safe.

4. Be aware of the ocean. If it looks strange, remember Tilly!

reaches the coast. That's enough time to alert people that a tsunami is on the way. Warnings go out on radio and TV. Sirens blare out along the shore. Everyone knows to head for safety.

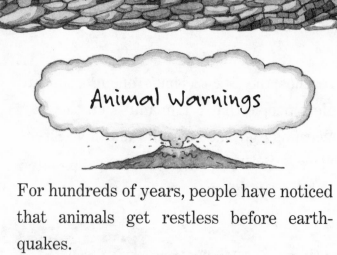

Animal Warnings

For hundreds of years, people have noticed that animals get restless before earthquakes.

Before the 2004 tsunami hit, there were reports that dogs refused to go out. Bats flew around nervously during the day. And flamingos and other seabirds flew up to higher ground.

On the coast of Sumatra, elephant trainers claim their elephants began to cry. Then the elephants broke their chains and headed for the hills.

Scientists wonder if someday we can find a way for animals to actually help predict earthquakes. And if they can predict earthquakes, they can also warn us about tsunamis.

4

Volcanoes

The word *volcano* comes from Vulcan, the Roman god of fire. When we think of volcanoes, we often think of cone-shaped mountains spewing out fire and ash. But volcanoes come in different sizes and shapes. Some are tall mountains. Others are cracks in the earth. Still others are gentle slopes with a crater on top. Volcanoes are a vent, or opening in the earth's crust. Hot melted rock erupts from the vent.

Volcanoes form near the edges of plates. When subduction occurs, the lower plate can be pushed into the mantle. The temperature rises. New magma begins to form.

Magma is lighter than solid rock. It begins to rise up into the crust. Magma rises through passages called *conduits* (KAHN-doo-itz). The pressure from the rising magma builds up. It forces the magma, bits of rock, gas, and ash through the crust. When they reach the surface, the volcano suddenly erupts. Magma escapes from the

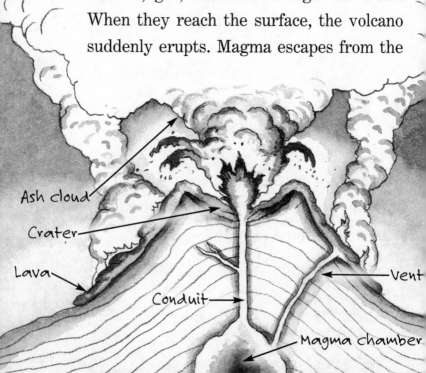

Ash cloud

Crater

Lava

Conduit

Vent

Magma chamber

opening of the volcano. When the magma hits open air, it is called *lava*.

Types of Eruptions

Not all volcanoes explode violently. The type of eruption depends on the lava itself. There are two kinds of lava. One type is thin and runny. Thin lava does not cause violent eruptions. It oozes slowly from the vent.

The second kind of lava is thick and sticky. It plugs up the volcano. Gases and steam are trapped under the magma. A huge amount of pressure builds as the gases and steam try to escape.

The gases behave like a bottle of soda when you shake it. Pressure builds up. When you open the soda, the pressure is released. And you'd better watch out or you'll get soaked!

What looks like smoke is actually ash shooting into the air.

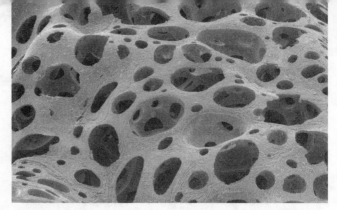

This shows magnified pumice, volcanic rock full of gas bubbles. It floats!

In a violent eruption, the mountain suddenly explodes when the gases break free. Clouds of gas, ash, and rock shoot high into the air. Poison gas, ash, and lava pour from the volcano. When volcanoes erupt many times over millions of years, all of these eruptions build up and form mountains.

Destruction
Violent eruptions can cause earthquakes, floods, tsunamis, mudslides, and rockslides.

56

People can suffocate from poison gases. They can be injured or killed as rock and ash pound down on their heads as they try to flee.

Carbon dioxide and water vapor make up much of the gases.

At times, the eruption creates a deadly mixture of fast-moving hot gases and pieces of red-hot rock. It can travel over fifty miles an hour! Scientists often call this quick-moving eruption by its French name: *nuée ardente* (new-AY ar-DAHNT), or "glowing cloud."

This deadly burst is also called a pyroclastic (py-roh-KLAS-tik) flow. Pyroclastic means "fire fragments."

In AD 79, Mount Vesuvius in Italy violently erupted. The Roman town of Pompeii was buried under six feet of ash. But what really finished the town was the *pyroclastic flow* that followed. A blast of hot ash and gas barreled down the mountain. It destroyed everything and everyone in its path.

 The town of Saint Pierre lay in ruins after the eruption.

58

The same thing happened in 1902 on the island of Martinique in the West Indies. Mount Pelée (peh-LAY) erupted. A pyroclastic flow roared down onto the town of Saint Pierre. About 40,000 people died in this terrible disaster.

Climate Changes

Volcanoes can change the climate. After a big eruption, volcanic dust drifts high into the sky and spreads out over the planet. The dust filters out the sun. The whole world feels the effect. Days become darker and colder.

In 1815, Mount Tambora on an island in Indonesia erupted. So much volcanic dust clogged the air that it hid the sun. Temperatures all over the world dropped. It even snowed in parts of the United States in June and July!

Shield Volcanoes

Shield volcanoes are very large. The top looks like a giant bowl or shield. When shield volcanoes erupt, the lava seeps out slowly and can travel for hundreds of miles.

Mauna Loa, Hawaii

Mount Etna, Italy

Cinder Cones

Cinder cones are the most common type of volcano. In an eruption, the lava is shot so high into the air that it cools into cinders. The cinders settle around the vent, creating an oval cone with a crater on top. A cinder-cone volcano doesn't usually get very tall.

Composite Volcanoes

Some of the most beautiful mountains on earth are *composite* (kum-PAHZ-it) volcanoes, or *stratovolcanoes*. *Composite* means "made up of different parts." These are steep volcanoes that reach great heights. They are made up of layers of rock, lava, and ash from many eruptions over the years. They have craters at their tops.

Composite volcanoes have thick lava that usually erupts violently. This makes their eruptions very dangerous.

Mount Fuji is a dormant composite volcano. It is the highest mountain in Japan. The crater on top is over 1,600 feet wide.

Over the years, many artists and writers
have admired this beautiful mountain.

Mount Fuji, Japan

Volcanic Activity

Scientists describe volcanoes as being *active*, *dormant* (DOR-munt), or *extinct* (ek-STINKT).

The biggest known active volcanoes are on Mars.

Active volcanoes are ones that have recently erupted or could erupt soon. Scientists think there are around 500 active volcanoes on land. There are more than 1,500 beneath the sea!

Dormant volcanoes have not erupted in a long time but could erupt again.

Dormant comes from dormire, the Latin word for "to sleep."

Extinct volcanoes are ones that have not erupted for thousands of years and scientists think will never erupt again.

Volcanologists

Scientists who study volcanoes are called *volcanologists* (vahl-kuh-NAHL-uh-jistz). They do research in laboratories. But they

64

also spend time at volcanic sites and collect samples of lava and gas. Volcanologists also check temperatures around the volcano.

Some volcanoes are very hot. The volcanologists have to wear heavy suits for protection. The suits are coated with metal to reflect the heat and keep the scientists from getting too hot.

Katia and Maurice Krafft were two famous French volcanologists. In 1991, they were checking a volcano in Japan. Suddenly it erupted. Their bulky suits prevented them from escaping. Sadly, both scientists died in the eruption.

A volcanologist takes samples on Mount Etna.

Paricutín:
A Baby Grows Up

In 1943, a Mexican farmer was working in his field. To his surprise, he spotted an opening in the earth. It was about 150 feet long. Then he heard a big noise like thunder. Suddenly the earth began to swell! Dust and ash came drifting out from the opening.

The farmer had discovered a baby volcano. Scientists named it *Paricutín* (pah-ree-koo-TEEN) after a local village. Paricutín didn't remain a baby volcano for very long. By its first birthday, it grew to over 1,000 feet tall!

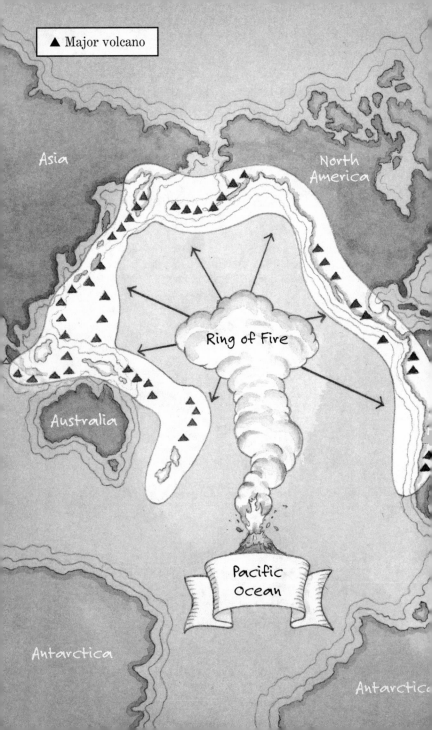

5

The Ring of Fire

The Pacific Ocean covers almost half the earth. Most tsunamis, volcanoes, and earthquakes occur in or near the Pacific Ocean. In fact, 90 percent of all earthquakes take place in the Pacific. They happen in an area called the "Ring of Fire." The Ring of Fire is a huge semicircle that runs along the edges of the Pacific Plate.

Japan is in the Ring of Fire and has more than 186 volcanoes.

   The Pacific Plate is a large plate under the ocean that is expanding. It borders many other plates. The plates often push into one another or pull apart. These movements cause most of the earthquakes and volcanoes in the Pacific.

Underwater Volcanoes

There are thousands of underwater volcanoes in the Ring of Fire. Scientists recently began exploring these volcanoes using underwater robots and small research submarines.

Underwater volcanoes can be tall mountains or openings on the seabed where lava oozes out onto the ocean floor. Sometimes metals erupt from the volcano. Instead of mountains, this creates tall chimney-like structures. The hottest are called "black smokers" because the metals that form them are dark. The water is very warm around these openings. Scientists have discovered interesting sea life around the underwater vents of black smokers.

Giant tube worms live in 176-degree water around vents —that's only 36 degrees below boiling!

Pillow lava is formed by hot magma streaming from a vent in the ocean floor.

Sometimes underwater volcanoes grow up past the surface of the ocean. This creates chains of volcanic islands. Hawaii, Japan, and the Philippines are all volcanic chains.

Mauna Loa in Hawaii is the largest underwater volcano in the world. It rises about six miles from the seafloor and is about seventy-two miles wide!

Mauna Loa first erupted over 80,000 years ago.

The Ring of Fire has produced volcanoes and earthquakes for thousands of years. Natural disasters in the past have caused big changes in the way the earth looks today.

Turn the page to learn about some famous ancient disasters.

Disaster at Chicxulub

Sixty-five million years ago, an asteroid crashed off the coast of Mexico, in what is now the village of Chicxulub (CHEEK-shuh-loob). The asteroid made a crater over one hundred miles wide.

Heat and flames from the asteroid started terrible fires. They burned from Mexico into what is now the United States. Dust and smoke clogged the air. Temperatures all over the world dropped. Plants and animals died by the millions.

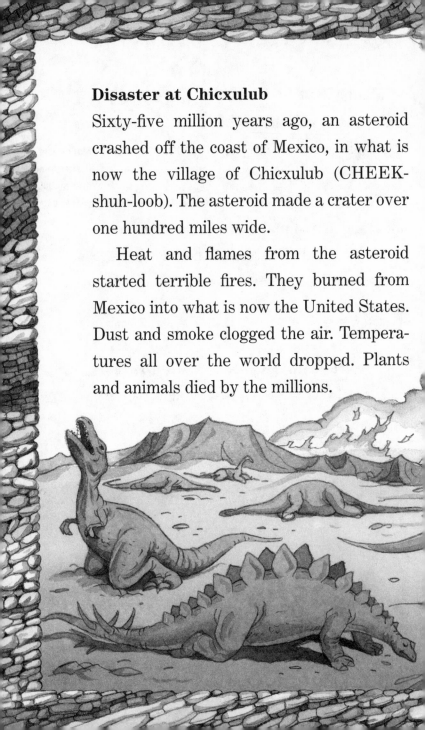

The impact of the asteroid also created terrible tsunamis that hit coasts from Haiti to Florida.

At about this same time, the dinosaurs became extinct. Today many scientists wonder if this gigantic disaster caused the extinction.

The Beast Under Yellowstone

Every day, tourists in Yellowstone National Park watch plumes of hot water shoot out of the ground high into the air. These are called *geysers* (GY-zurz), and they come from underground volcanic activity. The world's largest active volcano lies under the park. Some scientists call it "The Beast" because it is so huge.

About 600,000 years ago, the volcano erupted in a monster explosion. Entire mountains blew away. Whole herds of animals died for hundreds of miles around.

The volcano left a giant *caldera* (kahl-DARE-uh), or huge bowl-shaped hole. It has filled in with grass and dirt. Today most of the caldera lies under Yellowstone Lake.

Scientists think this gigantic volcano will erupt again someday...and they aren't sure when!

Toba: The Supervolcano

Toba is a large volcano in Indonesia. Scientists call Toba a *supervolcano*. Supervolcanoes have extremely violent eruptions. Toba's last major explosion occurred about 75,000 years ago. It was the largest volcanic eruption in the last 2 million years.

When it erupted, thick ash blocked the sun. The sky turned black. Even the rain was black.

For years afterward, temperatures dropped. Plants began to die. Most of the people all over the world died. Those who survived are your ancestors!

Today a beautiful lake lies in Toba's crater. Scientists say Toba is still alive. But not to worry—they don't expect Toba to erupt anytime soon.

The Lost Continent of Atlantis

Two thousand years ago, the Greek philosopher Plato wrote about a continent that disappeared. He called it *Atlantis*. Plato had heard stories of Atlantis. The stories told of an advanced culture destroyed by an earthquake and floods.

Today scientists are almost sure that Atlantis was actually the Greek islands of Santorini and Crete. A volcanic eruption and tsunami wrecked parts of these islands 3,000 years ago. Experts are uncovering cities on the islands. They have named the people who lived there the *Minoans* (mih-NOH-unz). What the experts have uncovered gives them clues that the Minoans did indeed have a wonderful and rich civilization.

The Destruction of Lisbon

In 1755, Lisbon, Portugal, was a beautiful city. On November 1, almost everyone was in church for a religious holiday.

Suddenly there was a terrible noise. It sounded like thunder. A large earthquake shook the city. All the great churches and buildings caved in. Fires raged through the streets. Shortly afterward, tsunami waves slammed into Lisbon's harbor. The lower part of the city completely disappeared.

Experts estimate that at least 60,000 people died—more than a third of the population. And in a matter of hours, most of the beautiful city was gone.

6

Landslides and Avalanches

In 1991, Mount Pinatubo (pih-nuh-TOO-boh) in the Philippines erupted. Huge mounds of ash piled up around the volcano. Ash drifted out over the fields. Rain turned the ash to mud. This created a mudslide. It began to rush down the mountain. People below were trapped under the heavy mud. Over 700 people died.

In 1970, a magnitude 8 earthquake

caused an avalanche in the mountains of Peru. The avalanche roared down the mountain at over 100 miles per hour. It rolled right over the town of Yungay. Experts think that up to 66,000 people may have died in the earthquake and avalanche.

This statue, along with four palm trees, was all that remained standing in Yungay.

Landslides, mudslides, and avalanches claim lives every year. These disasters cause billions of dollars of damage. What makes them happen? Can we do anything to protect ourselves?

Landslides and Mudslides

Landslides and mudslides happen when rocks, dirt, or mud slide down a hill or mountain. Heavy rain, volcanoes, or earthquakes

Houses in Laguna Beach, California, slid down a hill in a June 2005 landslide.

Bare hillside

can set off some landslides and mud-slides. Others happen when people cut down trees on the hillsides or there are wildfires. The hillsides become bare, with nothing to hold the dirt down. If it rains a lot, the dirt turns to mud.

Gravity is the force that pulls things down to the earth. Without it, we would float away like balloons!

Gravity (GRAV-uh-tee) causes the loose dirt and mud to move down the slope. Some landslides and mudslides move slowly, but others move quickly, taking everyone by surprise.

88

Mudslides usually happen after heavy rainfalls or snowmelt. If it rains after a volcano has erupted, lava and ash turn to mud. The mudslide that results is called a *lahar* (LAH-har).

The worst landslide ever recorded happened on May 18, 1980, when Mount Saint Helens in Washington State erupted. Before the eruption, there was a magnitude 5.1 earthquake. The earthquake caused a landslide on the north slope of the volcano.

The landslide tore down the mountain at speeds up to 150 miles per hour. It plunged into Spirit Lake. All the water in the lake was pushed out. Six-hundred-foot waves crashed into a ridge. As the water settled back into the lake, it pulled thousands of fallen trees with it.

But that's not all. The volcano's eruption melted snow on top of the mountain. The snow turned to water. The water mixed with the lava and ash coming out of the volcano. Soon a giant lahar slid down the mountain. It destroyed 200 homes, forty-seven bridges, and 185 miles of road!

Mount Saint Helens landslide

Landslide Safety

Landslides and mudslides cause twenty-five to fifty deaths per year in the United States. There are things people can do to protect themselves.

1. If you live on a steep slope, listen to the radio and TV during heavy rains.

2. Beware if mud starts to trickle down the slope. Watch streams to see if the water level suddenly changes.

3. Move to high ground, especially if you see trees leaning to one side farther up the slope.

4. If a slide happens suddenly, get under a table or another strong piece of furniture.

Avalanches

Avalanches are a mix of rock, snow, dirt, and ice. They travel quickly and suddenly down the steep sides of mountains. Avalanches happen often. There are about 250,000 a year in the Alps mountain range in Europe. France has held the world avalanche record for the past ten years. Many of the avalanches in the United States happen on the West Coast. For the past six years, Alaska has recorded the largest number.

Large avalanches contain lots of snow. The snow could fill twenty football fields ten feet deep. Imagine being caught in that!

The most dangerous avalanches are called *slab* avalanches. They form when a soft or weak layer of snow cannot hold the snow layers that cover it. An avalanche expert in Utah describes a slab avalanche as a dinner plate sliding off a table. Slab avalanches travel fast . . . more than sixty miles per hour. You could never outrun one!

Blame the Snowflakes!

Under a microscope, snowflakes look like stars with six points. No two are the same. When snow falls, new layers of snow put pressure on the snow underneath. This pressure makes the points on the snowflakes rounder. The crystals don't lock together as tightly. Gravity forces the snow to slide down the slope. An avalanche is on the way.

Avalanches increase when the weather

Magnified snowflakes

warms up or during big snowstorms. The melting snow or the new snow on melted layers makes the snowflakes unable to bind together. One layer loosens, and gravity pulls it—and everything on top of it—down the slope.

Earthquakes, rainstorms, and volcanoes can also trigger avalanches.

People can even set off avalanches if they disturb unstable snow. Most of the

avalanches that kill snowmobilers and skiers are accidentally set off by the people themselves.

If you plan to ski or snowmobile on a mountain, tell people where you're going. And *don't* go alone! Sometimes there are signs posted that say DANGER! AVALANCHE! Don't go into these dangerous areas. If there are no signs, look for cracks in the snow. Then listen for noises. The snow may sound hollow as you thump it. You may also hear the snow make "whumping" noises. If you hear noises like this, it's time to leave!

After an avalanche, the snow may get as hard as cement.

If it's too late and an avalanche is on the way, you will feel a strong avalanche wind. This is moving air pushed ahead of the avalanche. If the avalanche hits, there are still a few things you can do.

Avalanche Safety

1. Let go of any ski poles you might have.

2. Quickly tighten your clothing to keep the snow out.

3. If possible, grab hold of a tree or rock.

4. When the snow covers you, make kicking or swimming motions to try and work your way back to the top.

It's not likely you'll get hit by an avalanche. Each year, only about 150 people die in avalanches around the world. But always remember something else—information is your friend!

Rescue teams search for victims of an avalanche in Austria.

A Timeline of Some Modern Disasters

December 26, 2004—South Asia suffered a deadly tsunami. It killed over 300,000 people. The exact number may never be known.

November 13, 1985—Colombia suffered from a volcano and mudslide. About 25,000 died.

July 28, 1976—Tangshan, China, was hit by an earthquake while people slept. Over 655,000 people died.

May 22, 1927—Qinghai, China, lost about 200,000 people in a deadly earthquake.

September 1, 1923—Tokyo and Yokohama, Japan, lost about 140,000 people in an earthquake and resulting fires.

7

To the Rescue!

Skilled rescue teams from all over the world rush to help in times of disaster. Many teams are made up of volunteers who give their time and skill to help. Doctors and nurses set up tent hospitals to treat the injured. Planes begin to arrive with blankets, food, water, tents, and medicine. There are even teams that come in to rescue animals.

People skilled in finding victims in the ruins of buildings arrive. Engineers bring heavy equipment to remove rubble. And all over the world, people send money, food, and clothing to the victims.

Rescuing People

The first challenge the teams face is getting people out of fallen buildings. Rescuers shout through bullhorns to the trapped people. They tell them to tap on whatever they can reach. As the victims tap, a device called a "life detector" senses where the noise is coming from. Rescuers then try to reach the victims.

Another helpful instrument is a "search cam." This is a special camera that can take pictures through small holes. The rescue teams drill holes into the chunks of concrete that surround the trapped people. They guide cameras into the holes. The cameras send back images of the people trapped inside.

Some of the best rescuers aren't people. They're dogs! Dogs have a much greater sense of smell than people's. Rescue dogs are trained to smell victims trapped under buildings or even snow. One avalanche expert said that one dog is worth twenty people in finding an avalanche victim.

A Spanish rescue worker and his dog search for survivors in San Salvador.

Being on a rescue team isn't easy. Aftershocks can shift buildings, trapping rescuers under the rubble. There is always the danger of disease and infection from polluted water. Everyone on a rescue team works long hours and gets little sleep. Doctors often treat patients and perform surgery in terrible conditions. But the rescue teams are tireless. Their goal is to save as many people as possible.

Natural disasters involve people all over the world. Thousands can be injured. People lose loved ones, homes, jobs, and even their lives.

We can help in times of disaster. We can send money or donate clothes. We can think about the people who are suffering. We can remember that we are all part of a huge world, a world of wonder and delight, and a world of natural disasters.

Doing More Research

There's a lot more you can learn about natural disasters. The fun of research is seeing how many different sources you can explore.

Books

Most libraries and bookstores have lots of books about natural disasters.

Here are some things to remember when you're using books for research:

1. You don't have to read the whole book. Check the table of contents and the index to find the topics you're interested in.

2. Write down the name of the book.

When you take notes, make sure you write down the name of the book in your notebook so you can find it again.

3. Never copy exactly from a book.

When you learn something new from a book, put it in your own words.

4. Make sure the book is <u>nonfiction</u>.

Some books tell make-believe stories about natural disasters. Make-believe stories are called *fiction*. They're fun to read, but not good for research.

Research books have facts and tell true stories. They are called *nonfiction*. A librarian or teacher can help you make sure the books you use for research are nonfiction.

Here are some good nonfiction books about natural disasters:

- *Avalanche*, Nature in Action series, by Stephen P. Kramer

- *Time for Kids: Volcanoes!* by the editors of Time for Kids, with Jeremy Caplan

- *Tsunamis*, High Interest Books series, by Luke Thompson

- *Tsunami: Helping Each Other* by Ann Morris and Heidi Larson

- *Volcanoes* by Seymour Simon

- *Volcanoes and Earthquakes*, DK Eyewitness Books series, by Susanna Van Rose

Museums and Parks

Many museums and national parks have exhibits on tsunamis, earthquakes, and volcanoes. These places can help you learn more about those natural disasters and how they happen.

When you go to a museum or park:

1. Be sure to take your notebook!
Write down anything that catches your interest. Draw pictures, too!

2. Ask questions.
There are almost always people at a museum or park who can help you find what you're looking for.

3. Check the museum calendar.
Many museums and parks have special events and activities just for kids!

Here are some museums and parks with exhibits about tsunamis, earthquakes, and volcanoes:

- Hall of Planet Earth, Rose Center, American Museum of Natural History New York, New York

- Hawaii Volcanoes National Park Hilo, Hawaii

- Mount Saint Helens National Volcanic Monument Castle Rock, Washington

- Yellowstone National Park Idaho, Wyoming, and Montana

Videos and DVDs

There are some great nonfiction videos and DVDs about disasters. As with books, make sure the videos and DVDs you watch for research are nonfiction!

Check your library or video store for these and other nonfiction videos about natural disasters:

- *Amazing Earth*
  from Discovery Channel

- *Ring of Fire*
  from National Geographic

- *Tsunami: Killer Wave*
  from National Geographic

- *Volcano: Nature's Inferno*
  from National Geographic

The Internet

Many Web sites have lots of facts about tsunamis, earthquakes, and volcanoes. Some also have games and activities that can help bring some fun to learning about such serious topics.

Ask your teacher or your parents to help you find more Web sites like these:

- http://earthquake.usgs.gov/learning/kids.php

- www.enchantedlearning.com/subjects/tsunami/major/shtml

- www.kidscosmos.org/kid-stuff/kids-volcanoes-types.html

- www.livescience.com/forcesofnature/tsunami_history.html

Software and CD-ROMs

Software and CD-ROMs often mix facts with fun activities.

Here are some software and CD-ROMs that will help you learn more about natural disasters:

- *Earthquakes*
  from Discovery Channel

- *Volcanoes*
  from Discovery Channel

Good luck!

Index

Italy, 57, 61

Japan, 42, 62, 63, 65,
   69, 72, 101

Krafft, Katia and
   Maurice, 65

Laguna Beach, 87
lahars, 89, 91
landslides, 41, 87–92
   destruction caused
      by, 87, 88, 91
   safety in, 92
lava, 54–56, 60, 61,
   62, 65, 70, 72, 89,
   91; *see also*
   magma
life detector, 104
Lisbon, 82–83

magma, 24, 54–55, 72

Malawati, 45
Malaysia, 45
mantle, 24–27, 54
Mars, 64
Martinique, 59
Mauna Loa, 60, 73
meteorites, 41
Mexico, 66–67, 74
Minoans, 81
moment magnitude
   scale, 33
Mount Etna, 61, 65
Mount Fuji, 62–63
Mount Pelée, 59
Mount Pinatubo, 85
Mount Saint Helens,
   89–91
Mount Tambora, 59
Mount Vesuvius, 57
mountains, formation
   of, 27, 56
mudslides, 56, 85,

87, 88, 100; *see also* landslides
  cause of, 89
  safety in, 92

nuée ardente, 57

Oregon, 48

Pacific Ocean, *see* Ring of Fire
Pacific Plate, 69–70
Paricutín, 66–67
Peru, 86
Philippines, 72, 85
pillow lava, 72
plate tectonic theory, 26–28
Plato, 80
pollution, 47, 106
Pompeii, 57
Portugal, 82–83

pumice, 56
Pumsi, Nataya, 17
pyroclastic flow, 57, 59

rescue, 18, 45, 99, 103–106
rifting, 28
Ring of Fire, 69–73
rockslides, 56
run-up, 44

Saint Pierre, 58, 59
San Andreas Fault, 29
San Francisco, 34–37
satellites, 47
search cam, 104
seismic waves, 30
seismographs, 32–33, 47

Photos courtesy of:

If you liked *Polar Bears Past Bedtime*,
you'll love finding out
the facts behind the fiction in

**Magic Tree House®
Research Guide**

POLAR BEARS
AND THE ARCTIC

A nonfiction companion to
Polar Bears Past Bedtime

It's Jack and Annie's very own guide to
the world of polar bears!

Look for it October 2007!

Magic Tree House® Books

Other books by Mary Pope Osborne:

Picture books:

The Brave Little Seamstress

Happy Birthday, America

Kate and the Beanstalk

Mo and His Friends

Moonhorse

New York's Bravest

Pompeii: Lost and Found

Rocking Horse Christmas

Sleeping Bobby by Mary Pope Osborne and
     Will Osborne

First chapter books:

The Magic Tree House® series

For middle-grade readers:

Adaline Falling Star

After the Rain

American Tall Tales

The Deadly Power of Medusa by Mary Pope Osborne
     and Will Osborne

Favorite Greek Myths

Favorite Medieval Tales

Favorite Norse Myths

Jason and the Argonauts by Mary Pope Osborne
and Will Osborne

The Life of Jesus in Masterpieces of Art

Mary Pope Osborne's Tales from *The Odyssey* series

Mermaid Tales from Around the World

My Brother's Keeper

My Secret War

The Mysteries of Spider Kane

One World, Many Religions

Standing in the Light

A Time to Dance by Will Osborne and
Mary Pope Osborne

For young-adult readers:

Haunted Waters

MARY POPE OSBORNE and NATALIE POPE BOYCE are sisters who grew up on army posts all over the world. Today, Mary lives in New York City and Connecticut. Natalie makes her home nearby in the Berkshire Hills of Massachusetts. Mary is the author of over fifty books for children. She and Natalie are currently working together on *The Random House Book of Bible Stories* and on more Magic Tree House® Research Guides.

Here's what Natalie and Mary have to say about working on *Tsunamis and Other Natural Disasters:* "We kept thinking about all the people who needed help after the tsunami of 2004. We read in the paper about kids and grown-ups everywhere who raised money and sent clothes and supplies to the victims. The whole world pitched in to help. That is the thing about disasters. Sometimes they bring out the best in people. But what is most important is that we help people *before* a disaster. We're very glad that tsunami warnings are now in place in the area where the 2004 tsunami happened. These warnings might work even faster than the elephants!"